How To Finally End Toxic Relationships Once & For All

By Ricardo A. Black

Published by Ultimate Better World Solutions.

Copyright © 2014-2018 by Ricardo A. Black.

www.ubws.net

For other titles, turn to the end of the book.

This book is licensed for your personal enjoyment only.

Published by Ricardo A. Black and Ultimate Better World Solutions in New York City.

Visit online at: www.ubws.net

Dedication

To all those who are still seeking their ideal partner.

Special Thanks

To Lovina Bhavnani Akowuah, for sacrificing an entire evening to read, re-read, take notes on her iPhone, and finally participating in a very late conference call with me to share her eagle-eyed edits.

Lovina, I really appreciate your eyes and commitment to excellence, and to my success.

To Mercedes Ramos, for constantly pushing me to finish this work, and for going the extra mile by translating the entire manuscript into Spanish. I want to tell the world that I am filled with gratitude for all the support and encouragement you've offered, you valuable time, and lots of patience.

Introduction

In *How To End Toxic Relationships Once and For All,* I explained how I was inspired to start writing about relationships after tuning into an episode of the hit cable reality show, *Bridezillas.*

Without a question, my first viewing experience hit a nerve that compelled me to explore human relationships on a deeper, psychological level. In that episode the featured *Bridezilla* moved in and out of each scene like a human wrecking ball as her toxic attitude toward her family, friends, and future husband spared no one.

While *How To End Toxic Relationships Once and For All* was intended as a quick read on the subject of relationships, it's success has been truly astonishing. I became very interested in relationships and the psychological triggers that compel level-headed individuals to do things they would not ordinarily do in a healthy setting.

This completely revised version of *How To Finally End Toxic Relationships Once and For All* represents the version that readers all over the world has been asking for. Book number one whet appetites for answers that are delivered here in book number two. Some of the questions include:

• What really makes people behave as they do?

• Why do we blame others for conditions and circumstances in our own lives?

• How do we break the cycle of failure and futility in relationships to enter into more rewarding experiencing?

So, I thank you for purchasing my book. Find a comfortable spot, plug in some headphones, and get ready to learn how you can *Finally End Toxic Relationships Once and For All!*

1. Recognizing Relationships

Allow me to ask you a simple question:
Are you in a relationship?

It's not a trick, so please think about it and answer to yourself. This was exactly how I first approached the subject on relationships in a conversation with a caller on one of my weekly tele-conferences.

It was not a question about any particular type of relationship—platonic, romantic, or whatever—are you in one?

On that particular day my guest went to great lengths to explain how far removed she was from any sought of relationship. She had been devastated and hurt in the past and, according to her, went underground. She believed that she had successfully removed herself from any interaction with another human that could be defined as a relationship.

The Hermit

To be honest, I was actually taken by surprise at first, but after gathering my composure I shot back with the following response (catch a deep breath and try to keep up):

If you are living alone in an undiscovered cave, far under the sea, with no connection to the civilized world—you are lacking relationships.

To lack relationships mean that you do not have access to electricity; the internet access;

computers; telephones; televisions; or even a post office.

A lack of relationships also mean that there are no pets to maintain; no jobs to complete; no coworkers to communicate with; no enemies to fight; no friends to confide in. And, you are deaf, mute, and blind to the physical world.

Finally, having no relationships, you never learned to send smoke signals or morse code. As a result, you are definitely alone in the world, and in a very sorry state, at that.

For everyone else, relationships are all around us. Everybody is involved (to some extent) in a form of relationship. For the purposes of our conversation, I would like to bring attention to healthy relationships and toxic relationships.

Understandably, my guest needed a moment to formulate a response—which I assume is still being considered because she remained very quiet until the show came to an end.

Let's take a closer look at healthy and toxic relationships.

Healthy Relationship

A healthy relationship is any interpersonal connection that nurtures, uplifts, supports, and encourages health, happiness, love, success, peace, prosperity, and more money.

On a side note, notice that I actually included *money* in my definition because as I have deeply considered relationships of all sorts, it has now become very clear to me that every relationship is worth money.

Every relationship is either increasing or decreasing one or more parties involved. Your relationships have a monetary value. Look closely at your relationships and you will understand what I am referring to.

Now, back to healthy relationships.

A person can determine whether he or she is involved in a healthy relationship when all of his or her thoughts, energies, and resources are invested in building more memorable moments with whom ever the relationship involves. In fact, it is possible to be so overtaken by a blissful relationship that momentary shock is experienced when it finally becomes apparent that your type of happiness is not the status quo.

What are you saying, Ricardo?

To put it simply, in relationships, I do not believe that the majority of people are as happy as they can be or should be. Many people are either faking a smile; faking affection; faking contentment; faking orgasms; faking—faking—faking.

Yet, there are a few lucky persons who do not have to fake anything whatsoever. What about you? How would you rate yourself?

Are you one of the lucky ones?

Are you blissfully happy with the person or persons with whom you share your life?

If you had to change something, what would it be?

Change.

Change.

That's one of the hallmark undertones of this book. Healthy relationships remain healthy in part because the people involved are willing to change individually and together. Therefore, a great deal of effort has been invested in showcasing the importance of personal change and relational success. For someone who answers no to the "blissfully happy" question asked earlier, it may be time for change.

Are you comfortable with change? Or, do you avoid change like a plague?

Start by defining where you are at this moment in your relationships. If you are not blissfully happy in your relationships right now, you are probably in a toxic relationship. If you are not willing to change yourself as the times continue to change, you run the risk of becoming a casualty of social progress ,and may soon find yourself up the proverbial river of life without a paddle.

Toxic Relationship

A toxic relationship is any interpersonal connection that deprives one or more parties of the positive qualities of a healthy relationship, and promotes unhealthy, unhappy, and powerless feelings and emotions. A toxic relationship drains life and energy, and spews negativity at every opportunity.

Are you in a toxic relationship? Can you recognize the signs of a toxic relationship?

In my opinion, toxic relationships are like social vampires that suck and drain life-force, mental energy, and even financial resources from its unwitting victims. When in a toxic relationship or close to someone who is toxic, it becomes difficult to put on a sincere smile, because it simply feels bad trying to look good.

Although there are many tell-tale signs of a toxic relationship, here are a few common ones to look out for:

1. ***Gossip and character assassination***. A toxic person endeavors to find faults with everyone. A great deal of his or her time is spent criticizing others. They may comment on how you fold your laundry; the way you brush your teeth; the type of clothes you wear; and even the friends you keep. Do you know anyone fitting this description? That's toxic.

2. ***Devalued opinions.*** Sometimes, one has to wonder how they managed to survive before Mr. or Mrs. Toxic came along. Mr. or Mrs. Toxic don't ask for or care about your opinion and they are quick to silence your voice without provocation. As far as Mr. or

Mrs. Toxic is concerned, you do not have an identity because you do not need to be heard. That is toxic. Worst yet, your ideas are laughed at in the presence of your family and friends.

Could there be anything more horrific than to be belittled in front of the very people who most likely warned against Mr. or Mrs. Toxic?

3. ***Personal sacrifice***. You are constantly giving up more and more of the fun things you used to do so that you can spend "quality" time with your partner.

Do you understand what I mean?

Let's face it, there is nothing fun about sacrificing your personal pleasure for zero benefits. And, how can such time be considered "quality" time? Where is the quality, and for whose benefit?

4. ***Over-dependence.*** For whatever reason, you are beginning to feel as though you cannot exist or live without your partner.

   When one's identity begins to disappear to allow a partner's role to expand, it is a sure sign of trouble. Individually, you ought to know who you are, and become convinced of your own self-worth.

   Consider that your partner, who is now the center of your universe, lived quite successfully before you two became involved. And, so did you. You used to find time to stop and smell the roses (so to speak), and you led a vibrant and rich social life. Life can be vibrant and rich once again.

There are several reasons that a person might become entangled in a toxic relationship. For example, did it happen by choice or by chance? What other factors determine whether one experiences a life of bliss or toxicity?

There are definitely enough answers to each of those questions to fill volumes of books. For the purposes of this discussion I would like to focus attention on the role of family history in the propagation of toxic relationships.

2. Family History

One's family history can aid in determining what seems to be acceptable and expected behavior. From a cultural perspective, some parents either knowingly or unknowingly participate in and encourage physical, sexual, emotional, psychological, and substance abuse.

An individual coming from a household where all manner of abuses were condoned and accepted as commonplace is likely to enter adult relationships with similar unconscious beliefs. Similarly, one's comfort zone *may* include constant abuse, negative chatter, and irresponsible adult behavior that redefine moral standards and ethical practices.

Without having to get into specifics, do you get a sense of what I am talking about?

Family history is a predictor of future relationships. This may help to explain why some individuals continue to live with behaviors that contribute to his or her misery, yet when it comes time to select a partner, they tend to choose someone who is most like the very patterns that has made their lives difficult.

It is what I call the comfort zone syndrome: people are attracted to the very thing that they despise because it is also the only thing that they know. It is their norm.

This begs the question: do people expect the results that follow from the choices they make?

Better yet, should we be surprised when our relationships turn toxic? On the other hand, do we know where to send the "thank you" card for healthy relationships?

You Get What You Expect

When it comes to toxic relationships and their connection to family history, there is a huge difference between familiarity and fulfillment.

Unfortunately, most people growing up in abusive families learn how to cope and eventually expect similar experiences. Again, this is their norm. Normal is what is most familiar, even if it involves the most vile violation of human rights. Under such circumstances familiarity always trumps fulfillment.

In further considering this notion of familiarity, it is important to note that people tend to gravitate to what's comfortable and familiar. When a person achieves something desired, promised, or predicted, they are said to experience fulfillment. This can include acts of love, intimacy, support, protection, financial reward, and many others. When viewed through the lens of familiarity, fulfillment becomes a foreign concept.

What does all this talk about familiarity, fulfillment, and comfort have to do with toxic relationships?

Everything!

Vulnerable individuals tend to be most afraid of the unknown and unfamiliar. Therefore, while a toxic relationship may cause a more secure person to run for the hills, a vulnerable person may be more likely to embrace it with open arms; it is home.

3. Magnetized By Toxicity

Thus far we have discussed the differences between healthy and toxic relationships, as well as delved into the role played by family history in establishing familiarity vs. fulfillment in relationships. The big question I would like to address now is, "What makes a person vulnerable to toxic relationships?"

Put another way, why are some people seemingly magnetized for toxic relationships?

Have you ever known anyone who seem to jump from one relationship to another, each time claiming justifiable reasons for ending the relationship? Such a person may be experiencing a difficult time finding what they seek in the ideal relationship. On the other hand, who is to say that the long line of failed relationships weren't "the right ones", either?

On my teleconference calls and seminars, I often ask the following question to make a point:

Do police officers hang out with convicted felons at the local pub?

Are brain surgeons typically found sitting in the park playing chess with a bunch of strangers? Who do brain surgeons hang out with?

Do school teachers hang out with former students who hated going to class? Who do teachers connect with regularly?

The answers should be obvious: police officers hang out with other police officers; as do brain surgeons, and school teachers. Every person keeps company with others who are most like themselves. This is not a conscious decision that is made prior to leaving one's home. It is automatic.

I am an expert communicator, publisher, speaker, and presentation master. I don't have to ponder where my friendships are coming from. They just appear as needed, and they are always appropriate—in whatever form they may take.

Someone reading this book at this very moment may be saying to him or herself, "Ricardo, I respectfully disagree with that last comment."

My answer to that person (and you know who you are) is simple: this is not a matter of agreement; it's is a fact that will eventually be found to be accurate in your life, and you do not have to agree with everything I say. Its my reality."

We must all choose what we will believe, but just because some people may not believe in the existence of gravity doesn't mean they won't fall from the sky if they walked off the edge of a tall building.

The same is true for anyone in toxic relationships. Each person is subconsciously programed or magnetized to attract the most compatible relationships—whether good, bad, or indifferent. It's all you!

With this idea in mind, it now puts into perspective the answer to the question: "why do people become entangled in toxic relationships?"

4. Being Honest

Can we be honest (with ourselves)?

At this very moment, imagine that nothing else matters except your own honesty with yourself. No other person's opinion matters because your opinion is the only one that matters right now. You are all that there is.

Please shut the door to the rest of the world and recognize that you are the central figure in every aspect of your life.

Everything revolves around you.

Let's talk one-on-one.

How many times have you wished you could change your job; some of your friends and associates; or personal circumstances and conditions? For some, that's pretty much every day, but how about you? How often have you had these or similar feelings?

On a daily basis the conditions of life reminds us of how much we have accomplished as well as how much more we have yet to achieve. And, when our focus is placed on what we do not have, we can easily lose sight of all the good that already exists. Do you know what I mean?

Therefore, you must be willing to question yourself and your own motives—and be absolutely honest with yourself:

- What do you wish you could change about your circumstances today?

- What areas are you experiencing lack and limitation?

- What areas of your life keeps you up at night the most?

Please be honest with yourself.

Is it your job? Do you still find yourself leaping out of bed every morning, racing to be the first person at his or her desk, or have you lost your zeal for the work, people, and industry?

Perhaps its the balance in your checking account. Do you find that your money is already spent long before you have officially earned it? Are there more outstretched hands trying to extract money than those willing to write you checks and fill your pockets?

Maybe, its the person sleeping next to you every night; or your desire for constant companionship. Has the chemistry begun to wear off between you and your partner? Do you silently desire someone else? Do you make believe that you are kissing and hugging someone different than your partner when in the act of loving? Are you just as excited to see him or her today as you were when you first met? Does the sound of his or her voice still thrill you and make your body shudder with anticipation, or have you gotten to the, "Oh, it's just you" stage?

What are you lacking that would save you from your own situation? Did you know that you are your own savior?

As you read those questions certain images and memories should have sprang to mind. Certain conditions and people should be forced themselves front and center in your thoughts. If the images and thoughts represent a healthy relationship, then you are in a good place.

On the other hand, what if those same thoughts and images paint a picture of toxicity, depression, pain, and discord? Unfortunately, they are not going anywhere until you recognize the following truth:

Every person is currently experiencing the perfect relationships and conditions for him or herself.

Please repeat after me: "I already have exactly what I want in my life, whether I know it or not."

I do not expect that everyone will agree with this statement, at least not initially. Nevertheless, it is a reality that continues to play out every day in every person's life—regardless of color, race, creed, religion, or socioeconomic status.

This is so important that it bears repeating: You are already experiencing your perfect life. This includes the quality of your friends; the type of job you hold; the type of boss to whom you report; the address you call home and the neighborhood in which you live; your habitual mode of transportation; the types of restaurants frequented; the quality of clothes that you wear; your current state of health; wealth; and even your joy. Everything.

Here is another important statement that must be embraced and understood to achieve truly radical changes in one's life if so desired:

The conditions in your life are as they are because you are as you are!—Reverend Ike[1]

The first time I heard Reverend Ike proclaim that statement it was truly an eye-opening moment for me.

Let's put it in the first person:

---

[1] **Reverend Ike** (June 1, 1935 — July 28, 2009) was an American minister and electronic evangelist based in New York City. He was best known for the slogan *"You can't lose with the stuff I use!"* His preaching is considered a form of prosperity theology (Source: wikipedia.com)

"The conditions in <u>my</u> life are as they are, because <u>I</u> am as <u>I</u> am!

Put another way, you experience what you already are—inside the depths of your subconscious mind. That is why there is a perfect person for each one of us. And, from time to time, that perfect person will change as you change.

This universal law[2] guarantees that no matter who you meet, that individual represents your perfect match. They are perfect for you because you are constantly meeting yourself in other forms.

---

[2] There are seven Universal Laws or Principles by which everything in the Universe is governed. The Universe exists in perfect harmony by virtue of these Laws. Ancient mystical, esoteric and secret teachings dating back over 5,000 years from Ancient Egypt to Ancient Greece and to the Vedic tradition of Ancient India, all have as their common thread these seven Spiritual Laws of the Universe. Once you understand, apply and align yourself with these Universal Laws, you will experience transformation in every area of your life beyond that which you have ever dared to imagine. Source: http://www.mind-your-reality.com/seven_universal_laws.html#Part_2

Mental Equivalent

Personal experience has taught me that mankind is constantly attracting its mental equivalent. All thoughts, moods, and feelings fall under the category of *mental*. It's the total of your feelings about yourself. Your mental state is what you *believe* to be true about yourself.

It has long been known that the conditions and circumstances (physical appearance) of one's life are a direct reflection of one's own thoughts. In this regard, the physical aspects of one's life are *equivalent* to the feelings and thoughts that are habitually entertained.

Therefore, one's mental equivalent is the subjective idea of desired conditions, circumstances, and relationships in one's current experience.

On a personal note, my mental equivalents are constantly appearing in my world in the form people, conditions, good, not-so-good, and indifferent experience that perfectly match the *nature* of my mood and feelings. There is no facet of my life that could be expressed outside of this idea. This is why my personal relationships, business associations, and even my pet dog are perfectly suited to me. The same is true for every person.

In case you feel like fighting against this concept, its okay. I understand. Go ahead and make your argument. In the end, its' truth will eventually become apparent, too.

I did not always believe this idea that I am now sharing with you, either. Upon first being exposed to this truth I put up a major fight. In fact, I was upset and disturbed for several months—mostly at the person who uttered the words into my ear. Later, I had to chuckle at myself, because it occurred to me that my reaction was similar to someone having to contend with an addiction. The first step is to admit that there is a problem before real progress can be made.

Why should something as insignificant as this idea cause such disturbance in my mood? Well, to be honest, I felt as though my scapegoats in life were being set free. It was as though someone was telling me that the people whom I regularly blamed for the issues in my own life were actually innocent.

One must be willing to take full responsibility for the conditions and circumstances in one's own life.

I reasoned within myself:

"Ricardo, are you telling me that I cannot blame my boss for firing me because it was my own thoughts and actions that provoked such a result? I have to blame myself?"

"Ricardo, are you telling me that the reason why the bus operator pulled away as I ran to the stop was not due to him or her being mean spirited; but, it was due to my decision to sleep an extra 20 minutes that morning?"

"Are you telling me that the reason I didn't get the raise or promotion I had hoped for was not because my boss preferred another employee over me; that it was not because my boss hated me; that it was not because he or she secretly planned to derail my career? Are you telling me it was because I choose not to take the extra courses to improve my skills, or did not demonstrate initiative or brought enough solutions to the workplace?"

"Are you telling me that it was because I didn't manage my time wisely, therefore my employer wasn't going to promote an employee with an excessive lateness problem?"

"Are you telling me that the reason why I may have become stuck with the same vehicle because I didn't really *believe* that I deserved something better?"

"Are you saying that the only reason why I do not have what I lacked is because I have not effectively possessed it in my mind?"

Yes! That's exactly what I am saying.

Self-talk can be very inspiring and liberating at the same time.

This was upsetting for me because it was sort of my emotional insurance policy knowing there could always be someone or something on whom I could blame all the things that went wrong in my life.

This internal dialogue effectively amounted to being hit on the head with a stick to get my attention. Once the pain subsided it did not take long to make the necessary mental adjustment.

No One To Change But Self

This episode reminds me of the woman who shared her plan to change her partner so he could act more like the person she wanted him to be. It started when they were dating and everything seemed to be perfect. Privately, she lived and made decisions that were comfortable and served her own purpose, and so did he. Their lives existed on separate tracks, only to converge whenever they went out together. At the end of each date, they resumed their patterned lives, yet while together she noticed several behavior patterns that irked her. In her eyes she had to change him to conform to her way of thinking.

Isn't that how many relationships work today?

Not long after being married the woman appeared to change overnight. She was no longer the sweet, loving, patient type whom her husband had fallen in love with. Now, she had a new mission—to change him so she could be happier.

Fast forward two years into the marriage and they are seated apart on a marriage counselor's couch; each blaming the other for the ills of the relationship. How often do you think this scenario is played out in private counseling rooms around the world?

How many couples waste countless hours complaining about their partner's attitudes and decisions? How many people are biting their tongues to avoid conflict, while living a hellish existence in a relationship that hopes to place blame on the other party for all the shortcomings of the other person?

5. The Eye-Opener

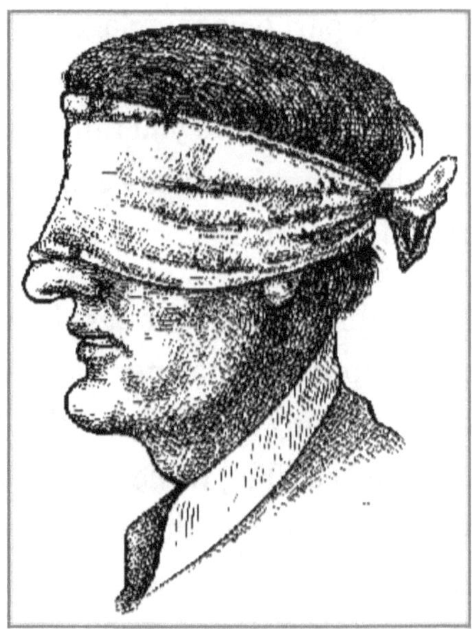

Several years ago I experienced my personal hellish experience. I was guilty of assuming that things could be better if only my partner could see things from my perspective. Let me tell you: there is no fun in trying to change another person, especially when they are made to feel like nothing they do is ever good enough. This was my experience.

After spending considerable time smoothing over hurt feelings that I created, a cordial discussion ensued. Somewhere along the way we decided that we should take out a blank sheet of paper and list the good-, and not-so-good traits about each other. Figure 1 provides an example of the perception exercise.

Figure 1: Perception Exercise

My Perception of My Significant Other

Positive Characteristics That I Like	Negative Characteristics That I Dislike

The exercise was conducted separate and apart from each other by an agreed upon date and time. After comparing notes, we learned that we shared similar character traits that were found to be troubling in each other. Although my partner was less vocal about her dislikes, here was proof that we reflected the negative aspects which the other complained about.

Wow!

Can you imagine that? What are the chances. I could have stopped here and accepted the data at face value, but I didn't. I simply couldn't believe it. As far as I was concerned it was a mere coincidence. Therefore, I contacted several other couples and asked them to humor me, and ask if they would conduct the same exercise.

Guess what? Similar results we attained. Each couple reported that they found the same positive traits and negative traits in their partners. I was shocked to learn that they were practically mirror images of each other.

Here was hard proof that I had married myself in a different form.

I was the problem.

It was me all along.

None of my irritations had anything to do with her; it was all due me. It was also a sobering thought as I came to realize that I was the secret source of stress and irritation for my lovely wife.

Yet, once I came to terms with the realities of our findings, I knew exactly what needed to be done to fix *my* trouble spots.

I had to change *myself*.

And, when I did, those troublesome traits disappeared from my wife as well. This was when I truly learned the meaning of the phrase, "You meet no one but you."

This was a powerful lesson; one that I would never forget:

The thing that commands your attention most in others signify its existence in you.

This eye-opening experience had such a dramatic impact on me that I immediately started to reevaluate all of my relationships. For me, this meant questioning everything.

Personal Magnetism

When it comes to one's personal magnetism[3] (your subconscious attraction power), external appearances are irrelevant because your subconscious attraction power is responsible for bringing into your life all the circumstances, conditions, and people that make up your daily experience. It is what makes you who you are; it is also what others refer to as *your nature*.

The good news is everyone draws unto him or herself their own conditions, circumstances, and relationships in a similar fashion. Essentially, we are a planet of individual, subconscious magnets that interact and share experiences. This is one of those natural forces

---

[3] Personal magnetism is one's attractiveness or interestingness that enables you to influence others. Source: www.thefreedictionary.com/ personal+magnetism.

that no amount of conventional prayer[4] can thwart. No amount of begging and pleading with a higher being is capable of changing this nature in man.

To change one's subconscious attraction power one must change his or her thoughts, feelings, and moods to match the ideal of the desired outcome.

It may seem silly to contemplate, but, some people have unknowingly tried to get around this basic principle for time immemorial.

---

[4] Conventional prayer is an outward, solemn request for help or expression of thanks addressed to God or an object of worship. Conventional prayer is what most people are taught to do when seeking to connect with a higher power than self. Unfortunately, most individuals are unaware that his or her constant thought process and mental attitude is their true prayer. In his book, *Resurrection*, Neville Goddard defined prayer as "the art of believing." This is the definition that is used in this book whenever the concept of prayer is mentioned.

Without an understanding of this concept, mankind will hopelessly continue to blame others for his or her lot in life. Yet, it's truths and powers are far reaching and omnipresent. As Reverend Ike would say, "It is so wide that you can't get around it; so high that you can't get over it; so deep that you can't get under it."

But, you can get inside. In fact, you have always been inside—at the center of this awesome power to create that which you wish to be; to do; and to have. Returning within is the key to changing one's external experience.

The Right Match

Have you ever felt that there was a perfect match for you somewhere out there? Many people believe that their ideal partner (soul mate) remains in the wild. They expect to meet that person with Mr. or Mrs. Right with all the perfect qualities they seek.

I am sorry to break the news, but you are always meeting Mr. and Mrs. Right. If you take a serious, candid look at *everyone* in your life, you will notice a pattern. But, you will only notice the pattern if you are truly open and candid about what you find.

Search Yourself

Let's take the category of friends as an example.

Suppose you have five close friends, each with distinct personalities and habits. While none of them are perfect copies of each other, Upon closer examination you may find that there is at least one defining trait in each friend that is also common in you. Since you are the common factor in all your relationships, if something appears in all your friends, it must be also in you. Can we agree?

How would you describe yourself? What traits do you and your closest friends have in common? Think about the good and the not-so-good traits as you describe them to the best of your ability. Here are a few examples to consider:

- Considerate

- Humorous

- Unselfish

- Adolescent

- Rude

- Philanthropic

- Stingy

- Punctual

Next, take a closer, more private look at your own traits. Are *any* of those qualities present in your friends also present in you to any extent? If you can identify these qualities in you and in your friends, then you have discovered the forces that bind you together. Alas, let me be crystal clear here: this is not an exercise in fault finding. It is merely a process of self-introspection.

Self-analysis is not fault finding.

There is no right or wrong answer to any of these questions because everything is subject to change as circumstances and conditions in your own life change. You are constantly changing, whether you know it or not. According to Science Museum[5], your body is constantly replacing old cells with new ones at the rate of millions per second. By the time you finish reading this sentence, 50 million of your cells will have died and been replaced by others.

---

[5] Science Museum (n.d.). Who am I? Retrieved on May 5, 2014 from http://www.sciencemuseum.org.uk/whoami/ findoutmore/yourbody/whatdoyourcellsdo/ howoftenareyourcellsreplaced.aspx.

Therefore, it goes to reason that if your cells are changing so rapidly, other things in your life may also be following a similar pattern, including your thoughts and feelings.

6. Change Your Mind

By now you are probably beginning to see how deeply rooted one's character is embedded in external experiences—whether good, bad, or indifferent. Therefore, putting an end to toxic relationships is not really about finding fault with or placing blame on others. It's not about them; it's all about you.

This means that once you have recognized aspects of yourself that you'd like to change it is easy to do so. It's literally as simple as changing your mind. And, when it comes to relationships of any kind, change is an important variable. I once heard a prominent speaker echo the words, *growth demands change!* It is absolutely true. To grow, one must be willing to change. The most important change is your mode of thinking.

Unfortunately, change is never easy to embrace or anticipate. Growth does not come easily, nor is it ever without pain. Yet, when all is said and done, the positive results of change typically overshadows its negative aspects.

Are you willing to change yourself to finally put an end to your toxic relationships?

Are you willing to do something you've never done in order to have something you've never had?

What are you seeking that has escaped your grasp till now?

Is a healthy, loving, caring, passionate, committed relationship?

Is it more money that you seek in your bank accounts; in stock bearing certificates; in certificates of deposits; more money to enjoy the good that you desire?

Perhaps you are seeking better health; to lose a few extra pounds; or to finally finish a marathon?

Consider your desires carefully and ask yourself, "What's holding me back from enjoying my desires to the fullest?" As you commune with yourself along these lines you will have the opportunity to accept or reject some of your own thoughts. You will notice a voice of dissent or encouragement as you consider each of your desires on a deeper level.

Listen carefully to your own thoughts because they will reveal to you the solutions to achieving your own goals. Have you noticed that I am constantly saying "your own"? That is because there is only one person who can truly effect the kind of change you ought to achieve: you, and only you!

Oftentimes, some people say that they want a partner who is loving and caring, yet he or she is unaware that they are withholding love and care from others. Or, perhaps they dispense love and care in measured amounts, though expecting their ideal partner to deliver unlimited outpouring of the same.

It is impossible to receive less than you give. But, you can receive more. Therefore, if you are not receiving enough in an area maybe its an indication that you have not given as much as you can.

What's the solution?

Love more, and love more completely.

Care more, and care more completely.

This means loving and caring without strings attached; without conditions.

The same goes for money.

If you want more money, you have to give it so yourself by seeing yourself as the one who already has more money.

The lack of money is an indication of a money rejection complex. Somewhere in the mind exists the idea that money is not good, or that you do not deserve money. At some point in your life you accepted the idea that money is dirty, or not important. It was not to be treated special. That idea was allowed to relax and take up residence.

Are you ready to finally end your toxic relationship with money?

To do so, one must recognize that money is very good stuff, indeed. In fact, money makes the world go round. It is currency, and it demands to circulate. Otherwise, it can cause financial constipation and other very unpleasant experiences. There is nothing that you desire that money cannot provide—including love.

I can almost hear someone thinking, "money can't buy love." Oh yes it can. Think carefully and be truly honest. Money must be embraced as the cosmic entity that it is. It has a personality all its own, and is subject to the same emotional disturbances that real people experience.

There is no amount of love that can overcome the lack of money.

We are still talking about finally ending toxic relationships once and for all. Anyone who disagrees should take this challenge: see how long your partner's love and affection will last without money. See how long it takes before he or she packs up his or her affections when your wallet dries up.

In America, it is common for married couples to divorce citing "irreconcilable differences"—otherwise known as unreasonable behavior. Specifically, an example of "unreasonable behaviors" as a main reason for divorce is when one spouse is dipping too much into the family's piggy bank for risky investments, pleasure or other things they disagree over[6]

Although on the surface it may appear that couples may be experiencing financial disagreement (which is true), the real issue is

---

[6] Baker, B. (Sept. 2013). *Main reason for divorce not adultery or 'straying'.* examiner.com. Retrieved on May 5, 2014 from http://www.examiner.com/article/main-reason-for-divorce-not-adultery-or-finances.

each person's relationship with money that may be causing toxic results.

I don't mind investing quality time here talking about money, because it is an area in which many people experience challenges. This is about making a change to the way you, me, or anybody thinks about our personal values, self-concepts, and self-worth. It is all connected to our external relationship with money.

Here's an example:

I used to work with someone who spent a great deal of her time complaining about her job. For some reason she complained about having too much work to do (as if it's called work for another reason); not having enough to do; not liking the people on her team; wishing she could have more vacation time; and, shockingly, she even complained about how much she missed work while on vacation.

Here was someone who clearly could not find a place to fit in. From time to time she also complained about her lack of her "lack of money" problem. According to her, there was never enough money left over after paying all her bills to enjoy and treat herself to something special. Her money was already spent long before her paycheck arrived.

This co-worker had an infectious spirit—a negative spirit. She would walk the halls hoping to find someone to share her problems with. In fact, she never seemed to be satisfied unless she could infect someone with her vile attitude and misguided perspective on life. She was becoming an liability as she diligently dragged down the company's morale, one employee at a time.

Eventually, her dismal attitude caught the attention of her supervisor, prompting a private chat with the human resources manager. That conversation resulted in her being placed on probation. Unfortunately, this new chapter only provided her with more reasons for which to complain.

She made no secret of her belief that her supervisor not only did not like her, but was out to get her due to jealousy. Obviously, she thought, he must be threatened by her vastly superior skills. Eventually, she was relieved of her position and ceremoniously escorted from the premises. Now she had all the time in the world to do the other things that her job was preventing her from doing.

I never saw her again, but given how close we worked and the countless hours of negative chatter that came from her mouth, I can safely say that she would not be able to recognize the true source of her demise.

She did not want to work an honest day for honest pay. And, her subconscious mind took every negative feeling, bad mood, and complaint as her approval to create a new reality. A new reality that did not include all the things that she complained about.

How did she convince herself (her subconscious mind) that her present conditions needed to be changed?

- She did so by consistently *feeling* bad about her job.

- She consistently *talked* negatively about her co-workers.

- She developed a negative *relationship* with money.

- She constantly *yearned* for free time to spend on vacation

- She *believed* that her supervisor was out to get her

From her perspective, everything that she expressed was real. And, because she spent so much of her emotional energy and feelings thinking about how unhappy she was in that situation, she created her own solution. She attracted the solution, which is no job. Now, she has no money, and lots of free time.

Do you know anyone like that? There are many people in the world who go to work everyday with nothing but bad feelings and negative talk in their minds and their mouths.

Yet, every story has a different ending, because somewhere along the line people change their thinking. Some people decide to be more thankful in the face of lack, which in and of itself creates more reasons to be thankful; thus, abundance takes the place of lack.

A mental shift is necessary to mentally replace a present condition with a new condition.

In the story above, the woman became filled with the feelings and moods of displeasure. She was full of the feeling of having no money. Therefore, she got exactly what she ordered through her *feelings*.

If you are in a similar situation you do not have to lose your job and experience a lack of money like my co-worker. You can change your present condition to whatever you want—starting right here; right now.

Ask yourself this question:

How does it feel to be the one who already have the good that is desired?

How does it *really feel* to be the person that you wish to be? I want you to really think about what you want.

- What kind of person would you like to become?

- Where would you like to live?

- What type of car would you like to drive?

- Would you like to fly first class, business class, or coach? There is no wrong answer; just your desire.

- How would you like people to treat you?

- How much money would you like to carry in your wallet on a daily basis?

- What sorts of investments would you like to own?

- How would you like your personal relationships to change?

- How many pounds would you like to lose in the next 90 days?

- Do you want to start writing a book you've been thinking about? (visit www.ubws.net/publishing for full support)

To achieve the good that you desire you must become completely intoxicated with your desire. You must start to see yourself as the person who deserves the thing desired.

Suppose you would like to have more money, but you don't know how to go about doing so. The most important thing you can do to bring this into fruition is to behave like the one who already have all the money that you need and want.

To achieve something better than that which already exists, one must be willing to do something better. It's simply not going to work if a new ideal or result is expected to occupy an old space or an old way of thinking. Something has to change.

And, its ok to admit that you may not have done some things as well as you could have in the past. Certainly, you have done many things very well, therefore you have a frame of reference from which to draw a picture of personal success and achievement.

Taking Responsibility

To finally end toxic relationships also means taking responsibility for conditions and circumstances in one's life at this present time. You have to recognize that you are fully responsible for everything that has transpired in your physical experience up to this point in your life.

Some of those experiences may be blissful and perfect. Others may not be worth talking about. Either way, you have to take responsibility for initiating the results you have achieved— whether good, bad, or indifferent.

The great news about all this talk about taking responsibility is that, if you can think it up, you can certainly think it down[7]. This is fantastic news, because it means you are not stuck with the stuff that may have unwittingly been

---

[7] This was one of Reverend Ike's favorite statements, and it bears repeating: "If I can think it up, I can think it down."

created through the misuse of the mind. This is great, because each one of us have a built-in "eraser".

Isn't it great knowing that you are not stuck with mistakes of the past? I know that I am elated to know that I can change my circumstances and conditions simply by changing my mind.

What about children who test the patience of their parents and guardians? Are they subject to taking responsibility for their own thoughts, too? Yes, they are.

While parents and guardians may offer suggestions and provide what may be perceived as ineffable wisdom, ultimately every child must choose for him or herself. And, that is the essence of taking responsibility for one's choices and actions. Allowing children to choose also means that adults have to keep their own emotions in check, especially when their lovable bundles of joy opt to follow their our path.

We are still talking about finally ending toxic relationships. Oftentimes, unhealthy relationships arise between parents and their children because parents may not think that the child is capable of deciding certain things for themselves. On the flip side, the child—while seeking his or her own identity—may rebel in the face of feeling stifled by mom or dad. Parents, if you want to put an end to the toxic relationship between you and your children, just step back and allow him or her to own whatever results come from their choices.

Beyond a child asserting his or her own independence, there are some parents who cannot imagine their child thinking for him- or herself. Well, guess what? They are always thinking for themselves. They have very active imaginations—just like you had when you were a child. One of the risks of suppressing a child's decisions is they will not be able to trust you as they should. They may not feel comfortable sharing their inner thoughts, feelings, moods, and aspirations with you—or anyone—who shows little to no respect for his or her personal opinion.

Do you really want to put an end to parental toxic relationships? Then, you must be serious about teaching your child all the lessons you can, while allowing him or her to make decisions based on what you've taught.

Every parent has to know the rate of maturity at which their child develops to ascertain when to relax restrictions.

As a child I often heard many reasons why following directions and others' opinions was the safe way to life. That's what every parent wants—to ensure the safety and well being of their children. Following the rules was not something that came naturally for me, though. Admittedly, I got into as much trouble as I made my parents proud. Now that I am an adult I am glad that I was one of the "hard-headed" ones. I am glad that I often butted heads with authority figures, because I needed to maintain my own identity. Sometimes, ending a toxic relationship means taking the higher road and allowing people to experience the results of their thoughts—good, bad, or indifferent.

Maintaining one's own identity is essential in cultivating an attitude of self-accountability. And, when you really think about it, individuals were never meant to live by other's rules or standards. If that were the case, there would be billions of clones, and only one original person.

As it is now, it is far better to choose one's own destiny and live one's dreams. That is why sometimes a parent or guardian may become offended when their offspring follow a different path. But, that's all it is: a different path. And, that path is completely controlled and navigated by the one who selected it. The one has no other choice but to take full responsibility for whatever may come.

In the final analysis, the only person that I can change is myself. You can only change yourself. Therefore, life can become much simpler and stress free once we stop trying to control other people's lives.

7. Growth Demands Change

A caterpillar will never know what it is like to fly through the air, sampling nectar from flower to flower if it is unwilling to change.

A baby can never evolve to experience the thrill of driving a sports car around a race track at 200 miles per hour if it refuse to become more than a baby.

So it is with everything and everyone in life: to grow, one must be willing to change. Change is not necessary unless something is brought to its end or conclusion, and a new thing begins. There is no other way to "end" or "start" anything without changing something. There has to be an end for there to be a beginning. It is just the nature of things., Therefore, to end a toxic relationship means that a newer, less toxic relationship is desired or ready to start.

What are you willing to bring to an end to give life to something new?

 Sometimes, one's toxic nature may cause a less toxic situation to end to give life to another, more toxic situation. Such an outcome would be tragic, yet, it is exactly what happens every day in many people's lives.

Let me explain further with an example.

Several years ago I knew a young woman (let's call her Mary) who was involved in an abusive relationship. Her partner, John, was not physically abusive, but he was verbally and emotionally abusive. John was verbally and emotionally toxic. After many attempts to improve the relationship and the way she was treated, this person decided to end the relationship. It was a difficult decision because she genuinely enjoyed his company, except for his verbal toxicity.

After a few months as a single person, Mary met Donald, who seemed like a breath of fresh air. He possessed all the positive qualities of her former partner, and more. As their relationship progressed, Mary discovered a side to him that was not apparent before.

On one occasion, an argument erupted that grew louder and louder. In an instant Mary was knocked to the floor with a swift back hand to the face. Donald's behavior was a shocking development which took her completely by surprise.

Several months later the same scenario would be repeated almost by clockwork, until finally Mary realized the truth that her social connections were pointing out all along: her relationship with Donald was growing more and more abusive and her behavior was becoming more and more reclusive.

Do you know anyone who is becoming more and more reclusive? It may be an indication that he or she is the victim of abuse.

Once again, to save her own life, Mary made the difficult decision to end her relationship with Donald. Again, she found herself single and perplexed—always wondering, "Why do I always get the bad ones?"

Not long after Donald was shown the door that Mary met Henry while commuting to and from work. Something about Henry resonated with Mary, and the two just seemed to click.

As was the case in her previous relationships, Henry seemed perfect at first. Although she kept a lookout for signs of abusive behavior she wholeheartedly accepted him as her man.

After seven months together Mary started noticing a glimmer of a drinking problem in Henry. With time the glimmer became a shining light that was impossible to ignore. And, as he drank more openly around her she began to experience his drunken wrath.

Once again, Mary found herself victimized at the hands of another lover to whom she professed her love—and importantly, who professed his love for her. This was her third relationship in a row that resulted in abuse—verbal, emotional, and physical.

It is very important to note that both parties claim to love each other, yet the abuses continue. What does this say about love and toxic relationships? Is it really possible to be in love with the person with whom you share a toxic relationship? Absolutely. Is love a limiting or enabling factor in toxic relationships? It is neither limiting nor enabling.

Love is just another detail when it comes to relationships, whether they be toxic or nourishing.

Although Mary bravely ended her abusive relationships to avoid further harm, she only changed external factors, such as the person sleeping next to her. To truly get to the root of the problem Mary need to look within herself to locate the source of the abuse that she herself is constantly attracting.

Let's examine what's missing in Mary's thought process:

• She did not change her thoughts.

- She did not change her system of belief

- She did not change her deep, inner, subconscious feelings about herself.

- Mary failed to recognize that she is a major part of her own problem.

Therefore, since she has not truly changed herself, she has not grown beyond the scope of her current problems. They will continue to follow her and reappear in various forms until she comes to recognize her primordial role in her own relationships!

Could it be that the abuse existed deep within her subconscious self-concept? Are there lingering fears about relationships that are possibly connected to Mary's current state of affairs? How else can it be explained that she continues to **attract the same** experiences regardless of the partners involved?

In math, we are taught that fractions are common when they share the same denominator. For example, 1/8, 3/8, and 5/8 are common because they have the same denominator: 8. Although the numerators (the top number) are different, they all have the same thing in common.

Let's compare Mary and her various partners to fractions:

Relationship #1	John & Mary
Relationship #2	Donald & Mary
Relationship #3	Henry & Mary

As you can tell, Mary is the common denominator in all her relationships. The numerators (the partners) may be different, but Mary remains the consistent figure in all three relationships. Therefore, it is reasonable to expect that the source of Mary's abuse in all her relationships is Mary!

To achieve something you've never had, one must be willing to do something he or she has never done. Therefore, growth demands change.

Repeat after me: *"Change is good. To improve myself and my circumstances I must be willing to change myself."*

8. Check Your Feelings

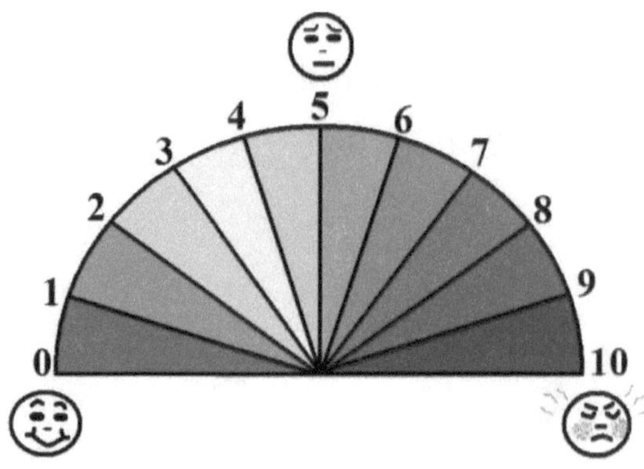

Relationships are all about feelings.

Feelings are one's emotional state. Your feelings represent your current state of mind and are connected to your *moods*. According to the *New Oxford American Dictionary*, moods are temporary states of mind. Moods and feelings are like the clothes that you wear in that they are very personal, and should be carefully controlled like any other aspect of one's personal experience.
Unlike physical articles of clothing, though,

feelings are directly connected to one's physical conditions and circumstances.

Did you know that your feelings are like magnets? That's why so many people attract people, conditions, and circumstances into their own experience that closely mirror their mood.

Have you ever observed a genuinely happy person? You couldn't ruin their day even if you tried, because their happy state of mind was so intense that it attracted a world of similarly joyful experiences in and around them. It would be nearly impossible for such a person to experience any extended periods of negative relationships, conditions, or circumstances unless they habitually harbored equally negative feelings and moods.

I am not saying that every day is going to be a bowl of cherries or a bright ray of sunshine, but generally, life will be a celebration. What's responsible for such a positive outcome? One's self-concept—a person's idea of him or herself that is constructed from the beliefs held about oneself and the responses of others[8] In other words, it's *how we feel about ourselves deep within the our subconscious mind.*

Your self-concept describes your self-worth and everything that you believe to be true for you. It's what we truly believe we deserve to be, to do, and to have. This deep feeling is so powerful, yet so subtle, that the person may not even know that it is there. This is partly the reason why one person may constantly attract certain circumstances and conditions, yet never quite able to escape what seems to be a definite pattern. My friend, the source of this pattern (whether good, bad, or indifferent) is all based on how you feel about yourself.

This all happened before, and it's constantly happening again and again for everyone.

---

[8] The New Oxford American Dictionary (2010).

Opposites Repel

When I was in High School we were taught that opposites attract; that positive attracts negative and electrons (negative charge) always bind to protons (positive). That's what the world of science has taught us.

In the science of life—my own personal experience—the exact opposite is true. Negatives and positives don't cooperate as much. They don't seem to like being in the same space. Opposites seem hell-bent on avoiding each other.

Earlier in this book the question was asked, "Who do brain surgeons and teachers hang out with." The reason why brain surgeons connect with other brain surgeons is because they have something in common. Teachers connect with other teachers; bus operators have a lot of friends who are also bus operators. The same is true for lawyers, politicians, bank robbers, priests, convicted felons, single mothers, financial analysts, and many others. Each person is naturally drawn to others with whom they share something in common. And this brings us back to toxic relationships.

Another example is divorce court. Consider two people bound together by the vows of marriage. Let's say that the attractive force that bound the two together was a shared love for art. Art, then, is the common denominator in the relationship. This couple may have met at a museum or an art gallery; or introduced to each other by mutual friends who also liked art.

Over time other aspects of their relationship blossomed, resulting in a shared commitment, loyalty, respect, admiration, and devotion to each other. Some how, somewhere, one (or both) of them made a choice that was no longer in harmony with the bonds that held them together. Perhaps, art lost its importance for him (it could be for her, too). He no longer wanted to visit galleries or to talk about art. He started to develop new interests. And, without this shared love for art, conversations at home became strained or less common. They said less to each other during dinner time; stopped visiting the same people (who also liked to talk about art); and they each started to do more things apart. The bonds became weak therefore they started to slowly drift apart.

Over time they no longer shared the same bed, car, or even the dinner table. Finally, one or both parties decided that it was time to call it quits—the relationship had lost its luster and had turned toxic.

Where there once was strong force of attraction (art), there is now a strong force of repulsion (lack of art). This relationship will not survive and must end in divorce. If not, the longer they remained married, the more tension (repulsion) developed between them.

That's the power of opposing forces. One way to fix this relationship is for both parties to change their magnetic charge.

Changing Your Charge

Marriage counsellors are well acquainted with relationships that has lost their attractive bonds. To salvage some relationships, counsellors utilize various strategies to engage both parties.

For example, Whitbourne (2012), recommended five principles of effective couples therapy, including modifying dysfunctional behavior, decreasing emotional avoidance, improving communication, and promoting strengths.

Modifying Dysfunctional Behavior

Oftentimes, the way that partners behave around each other is one source of their marital problem. Therapists may attempt to improve interactions by discouraging actions that can cause physical, psychological, or economic harm[9]. After it has been determined that either partner is safe and secure in the relationship, time-out procedures may be used to halt the escalation of conflict.

Decreasing Emotional Avoidance

As the level of toxicity increase in relationships, partners may avoid expressing important, private feelings to each other. This natural reaction can result in even greater distance emotional distance, resulting in a feeling of growing apart. To counteract this negative effect, partners are encouraged to share parts while the listening party offer attention and empathy. Sometimes, the less communicative party lacks positive feedback and reinforcement. With time the consistent expression of their true feelings will eventually draw them closer together. Here, again, we see

---

[9] Whitborne, S. (2012). 5 Principles of effective couples therapy. *Psychologytoday.com*. Retrieved May 13, 2014 from http://www.psychologytoday.com/blog/fulfillment-any-age/201203/5-principles-effective-couples-therapy

that reinforcement and empathy helps to build a bridge of commonality between the two parties. As the commonality bond is strengthened, so is the relationship.

Improving Communication

Communication is probably the most important skill a person can learn. In fact, 85% of a person's success has been attributed to their ability to clearly and effectively communicate.[10] Communication skills are not only important in corporate contexts, but are equally important in personal relationships, too. To truly experience a blissful relationship with one's partner, both individual must practice effective communication. This communication should be uplifting and encouraging; not be abusive. And, partners should aim for light hearted conversation, lowered defenses, less tension, and not take

[10] Black, R. (2011). *Cracking the Presentation Code.* Available online at Apple iBookstore; Amazon Kindle; Barnes and Noble Nook store; and Google Play store.

things too personal to improve opportunities for partners to express their true feelings.

Therefore, some couples may need a coach to guide them through the process of developing better communication interactions that results in more supportive and understanding relationships.

Promoting Strengths

Toxic relationships are prone to development when individuals pay more attention to what's wrong with the other person that what he or she may be doing right. The most effective therapists bring attention to areas of strength in the relationship and aim to redirect each partners' attention from negative to positive.

This helps to add highlight what's already working in the relationship, and helps to remind the parties of the importance of what they have together. Without this critical step it becomes easy to lose sight of the aspects of the relationship that are worth developing.

About The Author: Ricardo A. Black

Ricardo is a man of many talents. He is an author, publisher, marketing communication genius, credit and financial educator, real estate investor, and a dynamic speaker. His books cover various topics including communication, personal achievement, relationships, and metaphysics. His ground breaking bestsellers include How to Finally End Toxic Relationships Once and For All and Cracking the Presentation Code.

His prolific communication and marketing career has spanned over 20 years, collaborating with Fortune 500 marketing firms including Pfizer, Novartis, Amgen and others. Ricardo has successfully consulted in data analytics, pharmaceuticals, medical education, real estate, professional and consumer marketing, hospital, insurance, biotech, and many other industries.

As founder and Chief Solutions Officer of Ultimate Better World Solutions, LLC., Ricardo's purpose and mission is to help individuals, entrepreneurs and small business owners communicate more clearly to achieve their personal and financial goals by creating generational wealth through education, personal development, and facilitated real estate investing and financial protection. As a thought leader on psychology, science of mind and communication strategy, Ricardo is a highly sought after ghost writer and Assisted Self-Publisher. Think of Ricardo as where the podium meets the library.

Ricardo graduated from Ashford University summa cum laude with a degree in Psychology and an MBA in Marketing. When he's not motivating and inspiring clients, Ricardo can be found taking long road trips with his family, watching a Mel Brooks comedy, or bike riding.

Other books by Ricardo Black:

How to End Toxic Relationships Once & For All By Ricardo A. Black (First Edition)

The original best seller that got the world talking about ending toxic relationships.

How to FINALLY End Toxic Relationships Once & For All
by Ricardo A. Black
(Revised & Expanded Edition)

How to FINALLY End Toxic Relationships Once & For All is the completely revised and expanded version of the international best seller: How to End Toxic Relationships Once & For All. This is the book that will save your relationships—with your partner, spouse, boss, co-workers, parents, and even money! How to FINALLY End Toxic Relationships Once & For All may possibly save your life.

Cracking the Presentation Code

by Ricardo A. Black

The ultimate guide to presentations and public speaking.

Slips of Speech

by Ricardo A. Black

Everything you wanted to know about how to avoid common errors of speech.

Getting Started as a Publishing Superstar
by Ricardo A. Black

Everything you need to know about planning, writing, publishing, and profiting with your own book.

The Job Seekers' Survival Guide
by Ricardo A. Black

Practical and proven tools to ensure your success even in the toughest times.

www.ingramcontent.com/pod-product-compliance
Lightning Source LLC
Chambersburg PA
CBHW031141250726

48655CB00002B/785